HOW TO CURE A LEAKING PAYCHECK

GETTING OUT OF DEBT, MAKING MORE MONEY, AND LIVING A FINANCIALLY HEALTHY LIFE

By Elly Frank

All rights reserved.

Copyright © 2016 Elly Frank

This book is copyright protected. Scanning, uploading, and distributing this book via the internet or through any other means without the written permission of the author is illegal and punishable by law. Please, purchase only authorized electronic editions, and do not participate in, or encourage electronic piracy of this copyrighted material.

Although the author has made every effort to ensure that the information in this book was correct at the time of publication, the author does not assume and hereby disclaim any liability to any party for any loss, damage, or disruption caused by errors or omissions, whether such errors or omissions are from negligence, accident, or any other cause.

Information provided in this book should not be construed as legal, accounting, or tax advice. Should you have any specific questions or issues in such areas, please consult your legal, tax, or accounting advisor.

ISBN Numbers

ISBN-13: 978-1539766667

ISBN-10: 1539766667

Dear reader,

This book is licensed for your personal enjoyment only. It may not be re-sold or given away to other people; friends, workmates, relatives etc.

If you would like to share this book with another person, please purchase an additional copy for each person you share it with, or encourage that other person to purchase his/her own copy.

If you're reading this book and did not purchase it, or it was not purchased for your use only, kindly return it to the sender or delete it from your file(s) and purchase your own copy.

Thank you for supporting the hard work of this author.

Special Dedication

To anyone suffering from a leaking paycheck. To someone looking for ways of earning extra income and living a financially healthy life.

Contents

About this book..7

Demystifying the three notorious myths about debt................9

Payday should never be a day of sorrow. 12

If it has to be, it's up to you 17

Find some quiet space..21

- *Seven most common debt traps*............................24

Involve your household..27

- *How your household leak money – 18 most common ways*...28

Start by building an emergency kitty...............................34

- *26 things you can do to make more money*..................35

Organize the debts and begin paying them......................46

- *The 3 popular debt organization and repayment strategies*....46
- *Four other sources of funds to help you pay debts*............49

13 financially healthy and highly rewarding habits to adopt 52

1. Live within your income...................................52

   - *The four vital questions you must ask yourself before you spend money on any item*...53

2. Establish other sources of income, and even more......54
3. Budget for every coin you earn..........................55

4. Save and invest part of your earnings, that windfall, or that bonus..56
   - *Some of the most common terms used in the savings and investment world..57*
   - *Things you should put into consideration before saving or investing any amount of money....... ....59*
   - *Some secure savings and investment options to consider......62*
5. Avoid crowd-guided savings and investment advise........70
6. Only get into debt you can afford..........................71
7. Spend more on items offering you savings on purchases..72
8. Own your dwelling place...72
9. Shun the company of negative financial influencers......72
10. Never lend money you can't afford to live without......74
    - *Six simple safety measures you can adopt to help you lend your money safely 74*
11. Have an emergency kitty.................................76
12. Take good care of your health...........................77
13. Always give back..77

Summary...79

About This Book

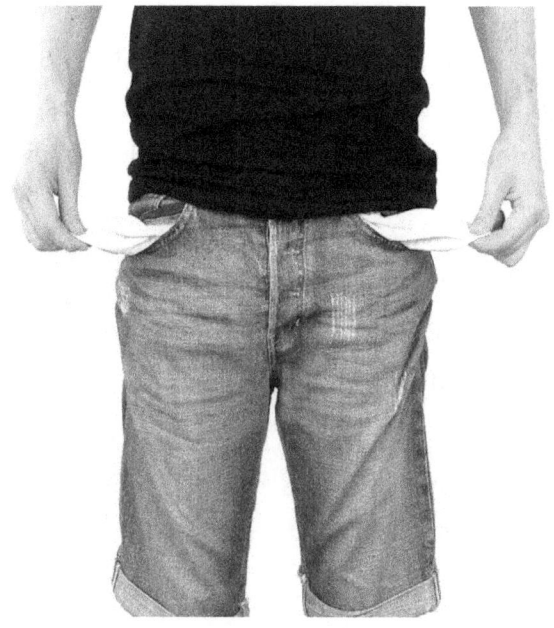

Do you suffer from a leaking paycheck? Are you debt-ridden and doubt whether you'll ever set yourself free? Do you earn some good amount of money but at the end of the day, week, month or year, can't tell where it's all gone to? Do you feel your earnings are never adequate to help you meet your daily financial needs? Is your pay-slip a beehive of loan deductions from numerous lenders? Do you wish to increase your income and start taking proper charge of your financial needs?

Are you in search of a financial miracle?

This book is your perfect answer. It's specially written for you. It has no hidden secrets, tricks, shortcuts, or even visualization exercises. If you believe you can manifest your way out of debt and start living a financially healthy lifestyle simply by thinking about it, put this book down and spend as much time as you can doing just that. Don't you think it's worth the effort?

Instead, this book details practical things you can do to take proper charge of your finances. It is a priceless guide towards living a financially healthy life.

> Read this book if you want to build something beautiful on the road towards your financial freedom.

Read this book if you want to build something beautiful on the road towards your financial freedom.

Demystifying The Three Notorious Myths About Debt

Being trapped in debt can be a stressful ordeal! The moment you're given credit by lenders or creditors, you are legally duty-bound to pay it back, regardless of any bad luck that may befall you such as job loss, falling sick etc.

Most probably, you've heard the below three notorious myths about debt. These myths are generally peddled by debt-ridden people. But it's time to demystify them, to help separate the precious wheat from the dirty chaff.

First myth

Its meager earnings that lure most people into debt.

Truth

It's never how much you earn, how early or how late you receive your earnings which determine how likely you get trapped in debt. It's your financial lifestyle - how you manage that which you earn. If you simply waste it away, you'll likely get lured into debt. But if you manage it prudently and create other sources of income, you'll keep yourself safe from the debt trap.

Second myth

Having a huge debt gives you immunity against job loss at the workplace.

Truth

Isn't this madness? Your inability to honor debt payments can hinder your concentration both at home and at work. You'll end up spending much time trying to figure out possible solutions to your debt predicament. And which employer do you think has time for an unfocussed employee in a world littered with overqualified job seekers? Summarily, having a huge debt, one that you can't comfortably service, will always make you vulnerable to job loss - as a result of your productivity suffering due to lack of focus and concentration.

Third myth

If the interest is low, borrow that money, even if you don't have its pre-planned use. You'll always find some good idea afterwards.

Truth

You are literally testing the depth of an ocean with both feet by borrowing money you have no pre-planned use of! However small or big the value of the credit is, it is a debt which must eventually be paid back. It's never free money!

Key Points

- *It's never how much you earn, how early or how late you receive your earnings which determine how likely you get trapped in debt! It's your financial lifestyle - how you manage that which you earn.*

- *Having a huge debt (one that you can't comfortably service) will always make you vulnerable to job loss - as a result of your productivity suffering due to lack of focus and concentration in your assignments.*

- *However small or big any amount of credit facility is, always it is a debt which must eventually be paid back. It's never free money.*

Payday Should Never Be A Day Of Sorrow

Nothing can be more humiliating on payday than being the owner of a leaking paycheck! And worse still, if you have no other source of income to supplement that leaking paycheck!

When evening approached, Godfrey left the office in a hurry. He couldn't wait any longer to withdraw end month wages from a nearby bank's ATM machine. As the head chef in a five star city hotel, he enjoyed a good package, earning more than double his colleagues'.

He boldly took out debit card from his wallet, but what followed after keying in his secret password was like a well choreographed Hollywood movie. Shock on him, the machine couldn't dispense any money since his account showed a negative balance reading! Thinking that perhaps that was an error, he hesitantly cancelled the transaction, removed his card and inserted it back. Weirdly, the negative balance reading still showed up, and persisted during the third, fourth, fifth, sixth, and on the final seventh attempt!

What do you do when you've done all you could to withdraw money you believe is in your account, but to no avail?

Still in shock and unable to come to terms with what was going on, he instantly grew wild and punched the ATM machine several times. Even those waiting at the queue could only watch from a distance as the renowned city chef changed jobs and engaged the rigid and cold money dispenser into a one sided fight.

How can you comfortably walk home empty-handed on payday? What would you tell your spouse, or even kids? And what sort of acceptable narrative would you tell your landlord?

> How can you comfortably walk home empty-handed on payday?

His first stop the next morning was at his bank where his worst fears were eventually confirmed. The negative balance reading which persistently showed up was the correct reflection of his account's standing!

Godfrey was trapped in debt. That month, he had secured mid-month advance credit from both the bank and from his employer, was paying three separate installments for personal loans from three different financial institutions. He was servicing two Sacco loans, was paying installments for a television set and a high end music system he had acquired via credit through two separate hire purchase companies. He had even exhausted limits on his two credit cards!

He couldn't believe the money sent to his bank account was never even sufficient to carter for the mid-month advance granted by the bank, hence the negative balance reading.

Your payday shouldn't be a day of sorrow, or a day to walk home empty-handed. It should be a day of joy, a day to celebrate all the thrills and pains associated with doing the kind of work that you do; waking up early in the uncomfortable mornings, returning home late in the evenings, attending those sweaty business meetings, overcoming the sometimes stressful work targets and deadlines, enduring all the sunny and rainy days, going through the uncomfortable traffic jams, etc. Your Payday should be a day of reward for all the emotional, physical, and psychological turbulence linked to the kind of work that you do.

Thus, to get full value for your work, you must therefore safeguard your paycheck. If you fail to do so and begin worshiping unhealthy financial behaviors, you'll always have minimal earnings to carry home each payday, or even nothing at all!

If not humiliating or hurting, how else would you describe the feeling of going to work, year in, year out, but at the end of it all, have nothing to show for all that effort!

You've got to do something! While your friends, colleagues and even relatives, some of whom earn less than you do, continue to do many things with their paychecks, your progress in life may seem stagnant, with increasing financial responsibilities but a decreasing income - if you own a leaking paycheck. And NO, you are not cursed! You are just in an unfortunate circumstance. And still, the sad reality is, you are never alone! Millions of people out there are owners of leaking paychecks.

While some owners of leaking paychecks have been forced out of their jobs due to their inability to take charge of their life, others have helplessly watched their cherished relationships go up in smoke due to their inability to take care of their loved ones finically. And in most unfortunate cases, some owners of leaking paychecks have ended up committing suicide in an attempt to run for cover.

Key points

- *Nothing can be more humiliating on payday than being the owner of a leaking paycheck!*

- *How can you comfortably walk home empty-handed on payday? What would you tell your spouse, or even kids? And what sort of acceptable narrative would you tell your landlord?*

- *Your payday shouldn't be a day of sorrow, or a day to walk home empty-handed. Payday should be a day of reward, for all the emotional, physical, and psychological turbulence you go through in doing the kind of work that you do.*

- *You've got to do something! While your friends, colleagues and relatives; some of whom earn less than you do, continue to do so much with their paychecks, your progress in life appears stagnant, with increasing financial responsibilities but a decreasing income.*

If It Has To Be, It's Up To You

Borrowing more, even at high interest rates to pay out existing debts and trying to run or hide from the lenders and creditors can make you a permanent slave of debt.

Ever heard of the popular aphorism *'if it has to be, it's up to me'*? Fact is keeping your eyes closed in a burning house doesn't help extinguish the fire! Closing your eyes will instead make you lose direction, making you vulnerable to be consumed up in the burning fire! You've got open your eyes and act swiftly to contain that fire, or let it consume you.

When trapped in debt, the initial step towards setting yourself free is to acknowledge that you are in a fix, and in need of help. Never sit back waiting for your employer, spouse, sister, brother, cousin, friend, etc. to push you towards re-aligning your financial off-tracks back to track. You must be honest with yourself, acknowledge that you are in a fix and in need of help, and bravely seek for that help.

Be bold enough and face the situation head on. Trying to hide or run away from your lenders is a game you can seldom win. And if you decide to just sit back and do nothing, then the debts will most probably outgrow your income, ending up subjecting you to never-ending financial humiliations.

A leaking paycheck can be managed, don't let it destroy your life. But you must be the one to make that bold move towards turning things around. You must step up and say enough is enough. Get fed up. Simply make a decision to stop living from a negative paycheck, from debts, from one paycheck to the next, or from relying on merger earnings, and choose the path of financial abundance.

> A leaking paycheck can be managed, don't let it destroy your life.

Never allow lenders and creditors to turn your paycheck into their shopping mall, each fighting for a space to deduct the limited money you earn. Well, it's undeniable the offers from most of lenders may always be tempting, but you must learn to manage your appetite of taking unnecessary credit. This way, you'll be blocking the lenders and creditors from scavenging for a space on your precious paycheck.

When trapped in debt, the process of getting back on your feet might seem physically overwhelming. You therefore need to prepare yourself together with your household, both physically and emotionally, for the uncomfortable journey a head. You would rather spend five years struggling financially, but thereafter, enjoy financial abundance for the rest of your life!

The clouds can hide the sun for a while, but not forever. Notably, the clouds can never replace the sun. Living a financially healthy life, littered with financial abundance should be your sun, and the debts trying to pull you down should be just but those temporary dark clouds blocking your sun's rays.

> You would rather spend five years struggling financially, but thereafter, enjoy financial abundance for the rest of your life!

If it has to be, it's up to you. You are never going to miraculously receive financial sanity and abundance without effort! The journey towards curing a leaking paycheck is one that not all who embark on successfully accomplish. It's a journey not for the faint at heart! But the good news is, once you find and hold on persistently to a proven debt exit plan, no matter how long it takes, you will eventually get back on your feet and sparkle again, financially.

Key Points

- *When trapped in debt, the initial step towards setting yourself free is to acknowledge that you are in a fix, and in need of help. You must never wait for anyone to push you towards re-aligning your financial off-tracks back to track.*

- *Never allow lenders and creditors to turn your paycheck into their shopping mall, each fighting for a space to deduct the limited money you earn.*

- *You would rather spend five years struggling financially, but thereafter, enjoy financial abundance for the rest of your life!*

- *You are never going to miraculously receive financial sanity and abundance without effort!*

Find Some Quiet Space

Find some quiet space, sit down with a copy of your paycheck, identify and capture all the details of exactly how much you owe - to whom, at what rates, and for how long.

Being trapped in unending debt won't not only give you sleepless nights, it can destroy your life, and possibly kill you! People are ensnared into debt from all the good and bad sources including: excessive spending (overspending), borrowing to spend on emergencies, loss of employment (source of income), development reasons such as building a house or purchasing a piece of land, payment of school fees, bad habits such as gambling, drug and alcohol abuse etc.

Today, the number of people trapped in debt is as ubiquitous as the many lenders and creditors that continue to open shops everywhere, day in, day out. Weirdly, debt is fun to acquire, but it takes blood and sweat to pay it back. And there is never something like *free money* from the lenders or creditors. You can't even get such *free money* from lotteries since you must first purchase relevant tickets!

The moment you've decided to put an end to your debt predicament, find some quiet space, *sit down with a copy of your paycheck, identify and capture all the details of exactly how much you owe - to whom, at what rates, and for how long.* Clearly, capture the amounts of that car loan, personal loan, credit card, mortgage, student loan, loans from shylocks etc. Without writing down these exact details and figures, it would be difficult to acknowledge that indeed you are in a fix.

Afterwards, identify the circumstances that drove you into acquiring each debt. Was it an emergency, a necessity, a want, or you simply got into that debt for the fun of it? You need to clearly establish the root cause of your debt predicament because if you don't know where you are coming from, it would be difficult to set up your direction and your destination as well. If you don't know what got you into that debt, paying it up would only pave a smooth way for you to run back into it.

Once you've identified the circumstances that drove you into acquiring each debt, classify them into two groups; *the good ones*, and *the bad ones*. If you borrowed money to purchase a house, a piece of land, or to pay school fees (or to acquire assets with appreciating values), then such would fall under the *good ones*. But if you borrowed money to purchase lifestyle-related items that you could have comfortably saved for, or wasted money on bad habits such as gambling, (or on liabilities with depreciating values), then such would fall under the *bad ones*.

Onwards, commit to shunning all the habits that drove you into acquiring the debts you've grouped under the *bad ones*, if you want to live a truly financial healthy life.

> Just because your payslip has a space to accommodate some loan deduction doesn't mean you should get the facility and use it to buy items you can comfortably save for

Just because your payslip has a space to accommodate some loan deduction doesn't mean you should get the facility and use it to buy items you can comfortably save for such as a new TV, a new high end music system, a limited edition watch, classy furniture, organizing a costly wedding, or going for a costly holiday in another country. Such would amount to abuse of that credit.

And do you know the common traps that lure most people, into debt? Take a look at the below **Seven Most Common Debt Traps.**

1. **Taking more loans to pay out other loans:** One grave mistake made by many people engulfed in debt is trying to take more loans, from different lenders (sometimes at higher interest rates), to pay out other debts. Easing one debt burden with another debt burden wildly growing common today.

2. **Unplanned debt consolidation:** Others take one major loan in pursuit of paying off other smaller loans. In most cases, such huge loans are mostly offered for an extended period of time. In the long run, the debtors end up paying the major loan for a longer duration of time, and sometimes even at a higher interest rate!

3. **'Top Up':** Lenders and creditors will always encourage you to *'top up'* your existing loans with slightly higher amounts, and even at sometimes slightly higher interest rates. A typical example is borrowing a five year loan to purchase say household electronics. After diligently paying installments for say two and half years, you are lured by the lender to *'top up'* the

existing loan, while encouraging you to use the little amount on top to purchase other stuffs. This is a common trap many people find themselves in. They keep on topping up existing loans to the point that they carry the loan burden into retirement!

4. **Unplanned borrowing:** The fact that you qualify for a loan or have an easy and quick access to a credit facility should not be an excuse for you to take it if you have no pre-planned use of it. Equally, you do not necessarily need to borrow money simply because you've seen your colleague or friend do so. This is a common debt trap that many people walk into with their eyes wide open.

5. **Investing more in liabilities than in assets**: If you buy land today, in five year's time, its value shall have increased. But if you buy a personal car today, in five year's time, its value shall have depreciated. Interestingly, you'll spend an equivalent of the car's purchase price to maintain it. Unlike assets, liabilities have minimal returns. Consequently, borrowing to spend on more liabilities than on assets often traps many people in unending debt.

6. **That wedding loan**: Some people are lured into borrow money to help them organize a memorable wedding.

Truth is, a good wedding should not propel the newlyweds into spending the rest of their married lives in debt. Many new couples across the globe have had their beautiful marriage dreams cut short because they either knowingly or unknowingly lured themselves into a wedding debt, but none of them willing to afterwards take full responsibility of paying that debt.

7. **That holiday loan:** Borrowing money to go for a holiday is an outright abuse of that credit facility.

Key Points

- *Being trapped in unending debt won't not only give you sleepless nights, it can destroy your life, and possibly kill you! Debt is fun to acquire, but it takes blood and sweat to pay it back. And there is never something like free money from the lenders or creditors.*

- *Find some quiet space, sit down with a copy of your paycheck, identify and capture all the details of exactly how much you owe - to whom, at what rates, and for how long.*

- *Identify the circumstances that drove you into acquiring each debt, then classify into the 'good ones', and the 'bad ones'. Onwards, you must shun all the 'bad ones' in order to live a truly financially healthy life.*

Involve Your Household

Fighting debt as a team (as a household) usually yields greater and faster results than doing so individually.

Ever heard that closing your eyes when it's raining doesn't stop the rain? Equally, that a cloudy day doesn't mean there is no sun? Instead of waking up one morning and issuing an executive order; cutting on all major family's expenses, simply call your household to a meeting, open up and explain to them the need of re-looking into family's expenditure and adjusting it accordingly.

Involving members of your family into re-looking and adjusting family's expenditure will get you better results, faster. If young children are part of the household, call them to the meeting as well, but you can spare them the finer details of the debt(s). However, you must try to make then understand why the changes you are suggesting are vital.

Did you know, involving young children in deciding on which items to cut back on exposes them at such a tender age on knowing the difference between the vital basic human needs, and the sometimes not-so-necessary human desires.

> Fighting debt as a team, as a household, yields better results, faster than doing so individually.

Fighting debt as a team, as a household, usually yields greater and faster results than doing so individually.

Next, it's vital to uncover **How Your Household Leak Money - 18 Most Common Ways.**

Below are 18 ways through which many people and households leak money:

1. **Impulse buying:** You walk into a supermarket and start purchasing items simply because its payday and you have money in abundance. At the end of the day, you realize you've purchased more of items you don't need

than those you are in dire need of. And what's the disclaimer on that purchase receipt? *'Goods once sold cannot be returned or exchanged'!*

2. **Purchasing more goods or services outside your budgetary allocation:** Also commonly known as excessive spending, this is one of the leading causes of money leak among many households! And on a lighter note, you should note that even governments are run on budgets.

3. **Spending simply to please other people:** You can call this unsolicited philanthropy. It may also take the form of spending out of peer influence. Spending your money on unbudgeted or unplanned items or services just to make you not fall out of place with your peers.

4. **Spending beyond your means:** Your mode of transport, where you live and what you eat should always be in alignment within your income if you yearn to live a truly financially stress-free life.

5. **Emotion-driven spending:** Spending out of rage, past disappointment, or simply to prove someone wrong or to show someone that you can afford that purchase. In most cases, the victims end up buying more of liabilities than assets.

6. **Spending on wrong investments:** Those investments that are hurriedly done without the input of relevant investment professionals. In most cases, such investments end up backfiring; eventually making you waste lots of money!

7. **'Mentor influence':** Spending on goods and services that your 'mentor' or someone you look up to may be in possession of i.e. a brand new trendy cloth or the latest sleek car, without giving due consideration to your purchasing power. You borrow money to buy such and after a few months, those items run out of fashion. You again shop for the next trendy item in the market. Such will always make you leak endless amounts of money.

8. **Delegating your spending responsibility**: You send other people to purchase for you goods and services even when you have all the time and the means of transport to do soon your own. You end up buying the items at inflated prices, and also incur extra costs on paying the person you have sent.

9. **Abusing debit and credit cards:** Withdrawing small sums of cash at the automated teller machines (ATMs), on a regular basis. You'll end up paying more for the associated withdrawal charges. Equally, withdrawing

money at alternative money providers, especially those charging higher service rates, exposes you to paying more charges at the end of the day. And exhausting the limit on your credit card makes you pay higher interest charges at the end of the day, hence leaking your hard earned money.

10. **Speed spending:** Many people, largely men, prefer spending in a hurry, without giving due regard to the value of items or services they are purchasing. Consequently, many end up purchasing counterfeit goods with low quality, which end up exposing them to health and safety risks.

11. **Corrupting a service:** Hiding in the name of 'a thank you tip', to be offered services you truly deserve for free. Well, to offer a tip is human, but to offer a 'tip' with a left hand and expect your 'purchase' with a right hand is an outright abuse of that 'tip'.

12. **The 'gift curse':** Unending urge to give out your hard earned valuable assets freely as gifts, even unto people who will never appreciate your reward.

13. **Excessive celebration:** This may be due to some great achievement, but celebrated beyond your means of income.

14. **Spending on avoidable emergencies:** Spending on sudden natural and or un-natural emergencies which sometimes may be within one's control i.e. sudden job loss and or sickness. One ought to be prepared for such rainy days by taking relevant investment or insurance cover. Equally, you should have an emergency kitty where you access money to help you during such emergencies.

15. **Phone credit abuse:** The emergence of smartphones phones has give rise to endless mobile phone applications which heavily rely on internet to function. And to access popular social media applications such as twitter, Facebook, Whatsapp, Instagram etc via these smartphones, you must have a functioning internet connection. Many people spend lots of time and internet surfing these social media sites, ending up leaking lots of money on phone credit. Also, continuous borrowing of phone credit makes you incur extra expenses especially if you get the credit at a fee.

16. **Those little things you don't take serious in the house:** The non-use of energy saving bulbs, non-switching off of electric gadgets not in use, buying household items at inflated prices due to not knowing basic prices of such items, leaving money in the pockets of dirty

clothes you are giving out for washing etc. These are hotspots for money leaks.

17. **Late payments of loans:** Doing this comes with the penalty of paying additional 'late payment charges'.

18. **Opting to pay interest on a borrowed loan for a longer duration of time, instead of paying part of the principal, or even all of it:** Whether the value of the loan amount is small or big, opting to pay just the interest, and not the full loan mount or even part of it is always an expensive undertaking in the long run.

Key Points

- *Call your household to a meeting, open up and clearly explain to them the need of re-looking into family's expenditure, and adjusting it accordingly.*

- *If there are children in the household, call them to the meeting as well, but you can spare them all the finer details of the debt(s). However, make then understand why the changes you are suggesting are vital.*

- *Fighting debt as a team (as a household) usually yields better results, faster, than doing so individually*

Start By Building An Emergency Kitty

Did you know that lack of an emergency kitty will often force you to view credit as your sole safety net? It's advisable having an emergency kitty of at least $1500. This will give you peace of mind as you go about repaying your debts. It will be that water-tight buffer between you and debts.

To build up an emergency kitty as fast as possible, pay up your debts in the shortest

> To build up an emergency kitty as fast as possible, pay up your debts in the shortest time possible, and have surplus money at your disposal, you must find creative ways of making extra money without turning to credit.

time possible, and have surplus money at your disposal, you must find creative ways of making extra money without turning to credit.

Well, today, there are endless things you can do to make extra money. Below, find a detailed list of *26 things you can do to make extra money.*

26 Six Things You Can Do To Make Extra Money

1. **Take and sell photos online**

    Websites such as iStock, Fotolia, Shutterstock, and Photoshelter offers opportunities for anyone with a great photo to sell it online. If you have a smartphone with good photo features, or any camera capable of taking great photos, you can put such into profitable use.

2. **Hire out your car, boat, motorbike or bicycle**

   If you have any of these, you can hire them out to close friends, family, or neighbors at a fee. You can also link up with taxi service providers such as Uber and use their platform to access clients, or even to offer your driver-services to them.

3. **Do you have a skill you can trade for $5?**

   If your answer is yes then head to Fiverr.com , create a profile and offer it. Fiverr.com offers a virtual marketplace where people sell and buy services from as low as $5. Are you a graphic designer? Can you edit documents? Can you produce short videos or audios? Can you write or review articles? Can you review books, songs or products? You have all these options and many more available at Fiverr.com. The beauty of using this platform is that you can complete a number offers in a couple of minutes and move on to others. And it's what you can do and the time you are willing to put into it which determines how much you take home at the end of the day.

4. **Run errands for other people**

   If you have means of transport, you can run errands for other people. Your friends, colleagues, or neighbors may be looking for someone to help them move out or to assist them pick up some items. You can also advertise your services on social platforms such as local Facebook groups and through Thumbtack.

5. **Create and monetize a blog or website**

    Are you an expert in a certain field or subject? Do you have a unique story or experience you would love to share with others? Create a blog or website and monetize it (put Google Ads or Google affiliate ads such as Infolinks or Chitika on that blog/website to earn you some extra income). Many people who have ended up quitting their well paying jobs to concentrate on building blogs and websites due to massive income they generate from those sites. Don't you think it's a cool way to boost your income?

6. **Charge some fee to take professional photos or play music at weddings or events**

    If you can take those professional photos, you can consider charging a fee to do so. If you can also play music instruments such as a violin, or have DJ skills, then you can consider advertising your skills for events on social platforms or through sites such as Craigslist, Thumbtack., gigmasters.com, weddingwire.com, and gigsalad.com.

7. **Take up mystery shopping assignments**

   If you can spare some time, you can consider picking up a mystery shopping gig and give feedback to the provider. To access numerous scam-free mystery shopping tasks, visit the Mystery Shopping Providers Association.

8. **Sell items you no longer use**

   You can assemble items you no longer use at home, or those that you don't find good use of, and sell them on Sell and Buy platforms such as *Olx, local Facebook Buy/Sell Groups, Craigslist, EBay* etc. Old electronics, used text books, oversized clothes, undersized clothes etc. The maximum amount of money you can raise doing this would depend on the value and quantity of the items you are selling, and the effort you are putting towards realizing success.

9. **Find avenues of earning more income from your current job**

   If you are in a commission based job, this is the time to work extra hard, or extra smart and earn more commissions through provided earning channels. And if there is an opportunity for overtime payment, consider maximizing on it towards earning more.

10. **Find a better paying job**

    If the nature of your job is kind of fixed on a certain salary scale, you can consider looking for a secondary job or a part time job elsewhere (as long as it doesn't conflict with your current job) to help you boost your income. Truth is, you are not going to work all your life. If you believe you are not being paid according to the kind of work you do and the value you bring to that organization, you should consider looking for a better paying job elsewhere. This would not only boost your current income, but also your lifetime earnings. And in case your employer might be unwilling to let you go, you can consider negotiating for a pay rise.

11. **Reduce your expenses**

    Reducing your expenses doesn't mean you are now resorting to living a cheap life. It means cutting back on those excesses in your spending. It means lowering your wastage. If you eat out often, this is the time to make adjustments and start eating at home, or carrying packed food to work place. That TV subscription you rarely use, or that monthly membership subscription to a yoga class you rarely attend can take a back seat for a while .Find what to cut back on to save some money.

12. **Can you spare time to take surveys and read mails?**

So many websites offer platforms where you are paid to take short surveys, listen to songs for a short duration of time, or read short-worded emails. A good example is Inbox Dollars. You'll join for free and you get $5 just for signing up. And once your earnings reach stipulated amount, you can withdraw via requesting for a check, or get it through your PayPal account. And once you sign up with them, you'll be getting other offers from other websites linked to them. You can also check SwagBucks.

13. **Become a translator**

If you are gifted with a spare language; bilingual or multilingual, you can consider doing part time translation work. Check Translatorstown, Peopleperhour, iWriter, Freelancer, Gengo, UpWork or Guru to find translation assignments. You can as well advertise your services online to access more clients.

14. **Find some freelancing work**

If you have problem solving skills or are a people person, consider pursuing customer service or a virtual assistant freelancing work on sites such as *Craigslist*, VirtualAssistants.com, **Fiverr**, Freelancer, UpWork, Guru and even on Zirtual. If you can write academic or business articles, you can pick up assignments on iWriter, Peopleperhour, Freelancer, UpWork or Guru. Depending on your skills and effort, freelancing offers opportunities for unlimited rewards. If you are skilled in design work, you can bid for jobs at sites such as 99Designs.com.

15. Can you rent your home or some spare room

Many people make good amounts of money simply by renting out their homes or spare rooms within their homes to tourists or travelers. To find interested clients, you can rely on sites such as vrbo.com, Expedia.com, airbnb.com, Jumuia travel, booking.com, roomorama.com, and Trip Advisor.

16. Take up a tutor job

Are you skilled in a particular subject or topic? You can charge a fee to tutor school students or interested adults within your locality. You can also find tutor related assignments on websites such as Chegg Tutors, and Tutor.com. Equally, you can consider teaching online courses via sites such as as Chegg Tutors teach.udemy.com, studypool.com, or Skillshare.

17. **Raise money through crowd funding**

    There are several crowd funding platforms you can utilize to raise money towards funding your dream ideas, or for any other cause. Kickstarter, Indiegogo, GoFundMe, Crowdfunder, Crowdsupply and YouCaring are just a few examples of such sites. The trick in raising money through Crowd funding is to write a compelling message that would lure people to donate towards your cause.

18. **Don't ignore those sweepstakes and opportunities to enter raffle draws**

    This might sound far-fetched, but remember, you never know what you can achieve until you try. But do this responsibly. Know when to pause, and when to quit.

19. **Join focus group**

    Focus group platforms such as focusgroup.com, mysurvey.com, swagbucks.com focuspointeglobal.com harrispollonline.com, ipoll.com, & inspiredopinions.com lists available opportunities in different select areas, and equally pays you to complete certain surveys. Typically, focus groups rely on select participants to solicit for feedback on products and services offered by brands, organizations, and businesses. This is vital in market research for the involved business entities.

20. **Sit or walk pets**

You can do this on a part time or full time engagement. You can decide on taking daytime or night time offers. The offers can be found on platforms such as *Craigslist,* Care.com, and dogvacay.com.

21. **Coach others at a fee**

Do you have an experience or skill in Yoga? Can you mentor others in areas such as public speaking? Are you experienced in advanced computer packages such as Excel, Spss or Stata? Can you train others on how to skate or how to play any game? Find interested parties and coach them at a fee. You can create a website or advertise your services.

22. **Make money from your craft**

Can you make those unique handmade items? Can you make jewelry or knit unique items? Can you draw or curve portraits? What unique craft do you have that you can sell to others? Use websites such as etsy.com or craftcoxes.com to access clients and sell such.

23. Be an independent tour guide

Can you devote some time to give tourists or travelers and in-depth tour guide around your locality, town, city or country? You can market your services on social media platforms and on websites such as vayable.com.

24. Buy select items at wholesale prices (discounted prices) and sell them for profit

You can buy toys at wholesale prices and sell them at kids' events. Equally, you can buy bottled water at wholesale prices and sell them at events such as a friend's wedding or at local parties. Just find any item which has good selling and profit potential, get it at wholesale price (discounted price) and then sell it at a profitable retail price.

25. Earn from Media ads

Is your home close to a main road or a highway? You can rent a space on the wall of your house for an erection of a media billboard at a cost. Equally, you can allow ads to be placed on your car at a cost. Check examples at freecarmedia.com. If you feel you look gorgeous, you can try modeling on part time or full time basis and make money marketing businesses and brands.

26. Can you risk being a guinea pig?

Can you risk being used in a clinical trial in exchange of money? You can check available offers on websites such as clinicaltrials.gov

N/B: Some of the suggested ways might not offer you the *get-it-quick* or a lot much money, but at least, they offer you avenues of making extra money in a more relaxed and fun way.

Key Points

- *Lack of an emergency kitty will often force you to view credit as your sole safety net.*

- *It's advisable having an emergency kitty of at least $1500. This will give you peace of mind as you go about repaying your debts*

- *To build up an emergency kitty as fast as possible, pay up your debts in the shortest time possible, and have surplus money at your disposal, you must find creative ways of making extra money without turning to credit.*

- *You can do unlimited things to raise the extra cash such as selling items you no longer have use for, cutting back on expenses, selling your craft, picking up freelancing assignments, and much more.....*

Organize The Debts And Begin Paying Them

There are several strategies you can use to organize the debts and begin their repayments. Detailed herein are three strategies you consider using.

The 3 Popular Debt Organization And Repayment Strategies

1. *Arrange the debts with the ones charging high interest rates on top on the list, and downwards - closing the list with the one charging the lowest interest rate.*

   First, identify the debt attracting the highest interest rate, and then channel all your repayments towards clearing it. Once fully paid, you then use the installment which was going to it, add it to the installment going to the second debt with the second highest interest rate until the second loan is cleared. Once fully paid, you then use the installments which were going to the first and second debts towards payment of installments for the third loan, and this goes on until you clear up all the loans.

The beauty of using this strategy is that it allows you to save more money. The mathematics behind this is that if you were to pay a debt attracting a higher interest rate for a longer duration of time, then you would end up paying more interest on that debt. Paying the same debt on a shorter duration attracts less interest payment.

2. *Arrange the debts in a descending manner – Debt with highest balance top on the list, closing the list with debt with lowest balance.*

With this approach, you identify the debt with the highest balance, and then channel all your repayments towards clearing it. Once fully paid off, you then use the installment which was going to it, add it to the installment going to the second debt with the second highest balance. Once fully paid, you then use the installments which were going to the first and second debts towards payment of installments for the third loan, and this goes on until you clear up all the loans.

This strategy is more useful if you have acquired some extra amount of money that you wish to throw at the debts. Once you clear the loan with the highest balance, you'll gain some confidence and momentum towards clearing the second, the third …until you clear all the debts.

3. *Arrange the debts in ascending manner – Debt with smallest balance top on the list, and closing the list with debt with highest balance.*

Here, you will channel all your repayments towards clearing that debt with the lowest balance first. Once fully paid off, you then add the installment going towards it to the installment going to the second debt with the second lowest balance. Once also fully paid, you then use the installments which were going to the first and second debts towards payment of installments for the third loan, and this goes on until you fully offset all the loans.

This strategy is equally handy if you are looking for motivation and building a momentum towards clearing debts.

Regardless of which debt-repaying strategy you decide to adopt, the most important thing is remaining focused and persistent. It won't be easy, and that's why you must persist to realize plausible results.

Four Other Sources Of Funds To Help You Pay Debts

- **Savings**

    You can use part of your savings to help you offset part of the debts, especially those attracting high interest rates. You'll end up saving more on interest. However, you should take the necessary precaution never to deplete all your savings towards debt repayment.

- **That sudden windfall**

    In case you've received some windfall (some good amount of money you didn't expect), use it to offset part of, or even all of your debts if it's possible. This will too help you save on extra interest charges.

- **That bonus or that hefty per diem**

    While it might be tempting to pursue other projects or even to go for a holiday with that hefty bonus check from your employer, it would be wiser using it to clear part of, or even all of your debts. If you've received some hefty per diem, you can save part of it and channel the remainder towards debt repayment. Having your monthly debt repayment reduced by some lump sum payment will hand you a lighter debt to manage and at a reduced repayment period. Instead of using that bonus money for short term gratifications such as going for a holiday, using it to offset your debt will hand you several years of financial freedom.

- **Perform a credit card balance transfer**

    A credit card balance transfer is simply using one credit card to pay off balance on another credit card, at a fee or for free. The trick here is to transfer the balances to credit cards that offer you zero or lesser interest rates.

You can also get a balance transfer credit card (a specially designed credit card to help you offset credit card balances at no, or favorable costs).

Key Points

- There are three strategies you can utilize to arrange and effectively pay up the debts

    - *Arrange the debts with the ones charging high interest rates on top on the list, and downwards - closing the list with the one charging lowest interest rate.*

    - *Arrange the debts in a descending manner – Debt with highest balance top on the list, closing the list with debt with lowest balance.*

    - *Arrange the debts in ascending manner – Debt with smallest balance top on the list, and closing the list with debt with highest balance.*

- *You can use your savings, that bonus check, or that hefty per diem to offset debt balances.*

- *You can also do a credit card balance transfer to manage credit card debt.*

13 Financially Healthy And Highly Rewarding Habits To Adopt

You were never born to merely exist and live your entire life paying unending bills and debts. There is a lot of financial abundance in the world which you too, should tap into and live a financially relaxed life.

Below are the thirteen financially healthy and highly rewarding habits you should consider adopting to live a financially fulfilling life.

1. **Live within your income**

    No amount of money will ever be sufficient to fully satisfy your day in day out financial needs.

Consequently, taking endless loans in pursuit of meeting such an illusion is a gamble you can never win. In the end, you'll easily get lured into debt, and possibly never have peace of mind.

Slow down on spending money you don't have and run your own financial race. Live the life you can afford, within your income. Learn to stay away from borrowing money to spend on items you can purchase from your income or savings.

Before you hurriedly embark on spending your hard-earned money on any item, there are four vital questions you must ask yourself to cushion you against unnecessary or excessive spending.

The Four Vital Questions You Must Ask Yourself Before You Spend Money On Any Item

First Question: Is it necessary?

Can your life go on smoothly without purchasing the item or service you are about to purchase?

Second Question: How urgent do I need this?

What's the level of urgency for the product or service you want to acquire? How bad do you want it?

Third Question: Can I afford it on my own?

In other words, can you afford purchasing that item or service without necessarily resorting to borrowing money elsewhere?

Fourth Question: Will I be getting value for my money?

Will you be getting value for your money? Will the item or service last long once purchased? Can you get the same product or service elsewhere at a better price?

If you can comfortably get a yes out of the four questions, that's a green light to purchase that item or service. But if you can't confidently answer all or at least three of the above questions, that's a red light on that spending.

Always be contended with the things you can afford. Enjoy them and most importantly, work towards improving your income to enable you afford more. Your day to day style of living should be a true reflection of your true income. Living within your income will help you thwart any urge of being lured into avoidable debt.

2. **Establish other sources of income, and even more**

The day you realize that no amount of money will ever be enough to help you meet your needs is the day you shall have finally graduated into adulthood. No amount of money is sufficient to completely quench the unending thirst of human financial needs. We all want more. We all desire to be in possession of the beautiful things this life can offer, yet these things are largely accessed financially.

The moment you establish your first source of income, working on a secondary source of income should be a priority. Even in the Bible, God established four rivers to water the blessed Garden of Eden. Why wouldn't He allow just one river to water Eden? Wasn't it a blessed Garden? You will always thrive in abundance when you rely on more than once source of income. And after securing your secondary source of income, work on acquiring the third, the fourth, …and even more sources of income. Have diverse sources of income. Never depend on one tributary, it might dry up sooner than you think and expose you to drought!

3. **Budget for every coin you earn**

Except for emergencies, lean to budget for what you spend your money on. I am sure you've heard more than a thousand times that you should have a budget for every coin you earn. Why don't you simply commit putting this into action? Living without a budget is like trusting a toddler to successfully crawl across a busy highway. It's that risky!

Budgeting will help you keep track of your earnings vs. your expenditure. It will help you put a right cap on your spending excesses. With budgeting, you'll stop viewing luxury living as some wish in a dreamland since you will always find some slots for your enjoyments, gratifying yourself as you go on with life.

4. **Save and invest part of your earnings, that windfall, or that bonus**

    It's never how much you have, how much you earn, or how early/late you earn your wages which determine the level of your financial success in life. It's how you put into use that which you have, or that which you earn.

    Truth is you are not going to work forever. Someday, you will be forced to leave the comfort of that business or that office through old age, retirement, job termination, resignation, on medical grounds (God forbid!) etc.. You must therefore, always put your financial house in order before that bleak day arrives.

    Learn to save and invest part of your earnings, that windfall, or that bonus. Your savings and investments will play a greater role towards helping you realize your life's dreams.

An age old tested savings principle is to save 10% of your net earnings, for a specific period of time, say five or ten years. Afterwards, carefully invest the saved amount somewhere safe where you'll earn a good interest at the end of any chosen period.

When you invest money, you put it to work for you. It should therefore be able to earn you a commensurate income at the end of the day. Significantly, you need to invest it somewhere where you can access it whenever you desire to.

If you save and invest part of your earnings wisely, you shall have provided in advance for your future financial needs and those of your family. And even in your absence, the continuity of your family shall have been guaranteed, financially.

Let's dig a little deep into savings and investments.

First, let's me take you through **Some Of The Most Common Terms Used In The Savings And Investment World**

- ✓ **Savings**: This is an amount of money kept aside, mostly in a financial institution such as a bank, possibly for future use. Savings may also mean the amount of money not spent on current expenditures.

- ✓ **Income**: Income is generally that which you earn from your investment. Examples of income include salary payment, coupons obtained from mature bonds, dividends payments from unit trusts/shares held, and interest earned from a fixed deposit account.

- ✓ **Risk**: Generally, risk is defined as a situation involving exposure to certain danger. All investments have certain elements of risk that an investor has to bear. There is an age-old financial maxim that *the greater the risk, the higher the reward.* However, when investing your hard-earned money, it's vital to keenly understand the risks you are being exposed to in order to make an effective decision on whether to commit your money or not.

- ✓ **Investment horizon:** This is the amount of time you take to invest in order to realize your financial objectives.

- ✓ **Return on investment**: This is the gross gain or gross loss that you realize out of an investment.

If say you invested in an item with a price value, then the return on that investment can be either a gain or loss in price of that item.

✓ **Net returns**: The total returns from your investment less operational, administrative, and other related charges. It's the actual profit or loss after eliminating accompanying costs/charges.

✓ **Capital gain/loss**: Simply the gain or loss that you make as a result of selling an asset/product at a price above/below the price you paid to acquire it.

Things You Should Put Into Consideration Before Saving Or Investing Any Amount Of Money

✓ **Define your goals**

Specifically, what do you want to achieve by saving or investing that money? Do you want it to grow? Or do you just want it to stay safe regardless of any profit? And how long are you willing to wait for it to mature?

✓ **Do you have an emergency fund?**

Before saving or investing any amount of money, ensure you have some cash reserve or some source of income to sustain you through the waiting period.

- ✓ **Have a clear understanding of the risks involved**

    Are you capable of bearing the associated risks? Can your life go on comfortably in case you unfortunately lose all, or part of that money? Deciding to invest part or all of your money is a serious decision in life, and such vital decisions do have accompanying rewards; negatives or positives. Are you able to live with the consequences of your decision to invest that money?

- ✓ **Do a research on other savings and investment options available in the market**

    Don't settle on a savings or investment option with minimal rewards when the best ones are just but a few minutes/hours/days of research away. Visit local financial institutions and or insurance companies to explore various products that have the potential to offer you better returns.

- ✓ **Read in between the lines**

Go through all the details of the option you want to settle on. Understand the terms and conditions of the offer. Know what you'll gain by holding on to your investment till maturity, and what you may lose by any abrupt withdrawal of part of the money, or of the entire amount. Investing in a product you have full knowledge of will always give you that precious peace of mind.

- ✓ **Establish the cost of your investment**

    Most investment products come with certain hidden costs. Weirdly, many clients only learn of such hidden charges at the maturity of their invested amounts, or when withdrawing invested amounts. Nonetheless, such costs, if any, are usually minimal and should not bar you from realizing your larger investment goals. But to be remain safe, always invest from a point of knowledge.

- ✓ **Have plan B**

    What do you do when your sole investment option fails to live to your expectation? Do you just walk away heart-broken, vowing never to invest any money again? Investments aren't matters of life and death. You may fail in one but succeed in another. The best investment strategy is to find ways of spreading/minimizing the risks associated with your investments. If you have adequate cash, learn to diversify your investments.

Next, let me take you through **Some Secure Savings And Investment Options to Consider**

- ❖ **Buy shares in the stock market**

    Shares are issued by companies in bid to raise capital from investors. The moment you buy any company's share, you become its shareholder, entitling you to the company's share of any dividends it declares and pays out. Across the globe, people buy shares of various listed companies in hope that price increase in future. Others make their purchases in pursuit of dividend payments, or as a shield against inflation.

Notably, listed companies pay dividends out of profits they make (if any). In some instances, listed companies may decide to re-invest their profits into the business.

When you own any company's shares, you have an option of selling them the moment the prices of the shares increase in value, or hold on when prices are low. And when a company is faced with liquidation but you still own part of its shares, you are rightfully entitled to its remaining assets; but only after all its creditors have been settled.

Investing in shares best suits people who can forecast the future performances/behaviors of listed companies. However, with good advice from trustworthy stockbrokers or investment advisers, you can take a stab too. There is an old-aged adage that *you lose 100% of chances you fail to take*. Most people fear investing their hard-earned proceeds in the stock market due to fear of unknown. This has consequently give room to a small portion of investors who are currently reaping heavy returns from various stock markets across the globe.

- ❖ **Open a fixed deposit account**

    This is another exciting option offered by several financial institutions. They allow you to deposit/invest a specific amount of money at an agreed interest rate, for a specific duration of time.

    This option may be better than merely opening a savings account since it has better returns on the saved amount. However, you will be required to deposit your money for a specific period of time, without withdrawing any portion of it. In return, your money will yield some interest payable at the end of the agreed period.

    You can consider putting your money in a fixed deposit account if you have no urgent or immediate use of it. And before doing that, carefully go through the offer and properly understand the pros and cons of keeping your there. It's advisable comparing offers from different financial institutions to get the best deal for your money.

- **Invest in a structured deposit**

    Just like its name, a structured deposit is a deposit but with an investment product. A structured deposit is different from fixed deposit account since it offers potential for higher returns. But on the other hand, it has higher associated risks such as the possibility of receiving lower amounts than your expectation. The returns on structured deposits depend on the performance of assets/products which they are invested in which include shares, bonds, and other fixed income securities etc.

    You will receive the principal amount you have invested in a structured deposit plus the interest as long as you do not withdraw it before maturity; provided the financial institution does not negate on the deal. Therefore, the credit risk of the financial institution holding your deposit plays a significant role in gauging the quality of returns in a structured deposit.

- **Invest in bonds**

    A bond is a form of borrowing. It's a debt security issued by a borrower i.e. a government or a company seeking to raise funds from the financial stock market.

A bond is classified as a fixed income security; it pays a steady flow of income at stipulated intervals throughout its life. Bonds are usually offered for a period of more than ten years (and sometimes even less). Other fixed income securities are Bills (debt securities maturing in less than one year), and Notes (debt securities maturing between one to ten years).

The life or duration of a bond is referred to as its tenure, and the interest from bonds are known as coupons. The rates of coupons are expressed as a percentage of the principal amounts, widely known as face values or par values.

There are certain bonds which do not offer coupon payments at all. They are known as zero-coupon bonds. The prices of zero-coupon bonds are mostly discounted of the bonds' par values. i.e. a zero-coupon bond of say $10,000 par value is issued for 10 years at $7000. It means that you will be paying $7000 for a bond which will be worth $10,000 in ten years.

The prices of bonds are usually quoted as a percentage of the par value i.e. a bond of 110% or a bond of 80%. Once a bond matures, it is redeemed at a face value, with those holding the bonds being paid one hundred percent of the face value.

Before you invest in any bond, understand the offer by carefully going through the terms and conditions. Read in between the lines and know what you are gaining. Keenly analyze the expected performance of the bond during the projected period. Possibly, you may involve services of a trusted financial advisor, or you can as well carry out the analysis on your own (if you have the capacity to).

Note, it's the credit quality of the issuer of a bond which determines the quality of the bond's performance. Mostly, bonds of higher qualities are issued by governments. Companies or institutions linked to governments such as banks also offer quality bonds. However, when investing in bonds offered by corporate entities, settle on those from good-rated corporate.

❖ **Invest in unit trusts**

A unit trust or unit fund is another favorable investment option offered by financial institutions and insurance companies. In unit trusts, your money is pooled together with money from other investors, and thereafter, cautiously invested by the relevant institution in a portfolio of assets according to the fund's declared investment goals and best fitting investment approaches. Unit trusts are mostly managed by experienced fund managers and operate on a trust structure.

The price of each unit correlates to the fund's net asset value. It is determined by dividing the current market value of the fund's net assets by the number of outstanding units. Your main gain from investing in unit trusts is realized when the price of the unit rises above the initial price you paid. Notably, unit trusts do pay dividends at certain stipulated times.

The beauty of investing in unit trusts is that it gives you a safer avenue for investing in a diversified range of assets, thus minimizing your risk exposure. It also grants you a secure access to markets or assets which may be more costly if you were to purchase them on your own. If you would love to own shares in the stock market, but lack the necessary know-how, you can test out with investing in unit trusts.

Unit trusts offer you flexible options to choose from. If you want total safety for your invested money, you should consider settling on unit trusts with capital preservation and income generation. Here, it is the investment banks or insurance companies who bear the associated risks. But if you want more appreciation of your money and are willing to accept greater risks, you can settle on funds inclined towards helping your invested money grow.

❖ **Re-invest in business (if you have one)**

When you feel satisfied with the returns from your business, the least you can do is to plough back all, or part of the profits into it. By doing so, you'll be positioning the business for an increased production, and possibly more output.

❖ **Be an angel investor**

Do you have a keen eye for identifying those startups with good future potential growth or good future returns? Today, there are endless startups looking for either financial or technical support.

You can identify one which looks promising, invest in it, and reap sweet rewards later after it has stabilized.

This should close the discussion on savings and investment. Let's therefore proceed with the 13 financially healthy and highly rewarding habits to consider adopting.

5. **Avoid crowd-guided savings and investment advise**

    There is growing pile of wrong financial advise out there emanating from 'financial experts' whose education backgrounds and experiences lie in other fields. Today, many financial and investment institutions are more profit driven, they care little about their clients' wellbeing. You must therefore seek for savings or investment advice from the right place or right persons. Anyway, why would you sacrifice part of your earnings for all those five, ten or twenty years, only to end up losing it in a bad investment? You must safeguard your savings and investments from avoidable potential losses.

    That everyone in your office is excited and rushing towards investing in certain shares should not be an excuse for you to follow that path without any sound financial or investment advice.

6. **Only get into debt you can afford**

You've endlessly heard that *you should never test the depth of a river with both feet*. Do you think you can have a comfortable sleep, or move around peacefully knowing that you used your car, house, business, or some precious household item as collateral to a credit facility you've defaulted on, with no possible signs of being able to pay up?

Naturally, borrowing money is a symbol of "incompleteness" and may literally turn you into a master (if someone owes you), or a slave (if you owe someone). It's a two edged sword. If you must borrow money, seek for an amount you can comfortably pay back. As an example, it's not bad getting into debt to purchase items with appreciating values, or to put in a viable business venture.

For purchase of assets with non-increasing values, you should save towards acquiring them, or purchase them from your income. Learn to manage your appetite for taking loans unnecessarily as such might trap you into the bottomless pit of debt. Debt isn't bad, but unplanned borrowing is like poison to a nicely prepared meal!

7. **Spend more on items offering you savings on purchases**

   Why would you want to buy a new television set from a high end retailer when your next door neighbor who is relocating to another country is offering a similar one month old TV for sale at half the original price? Must you be taking lunch every day at that hotel with highly priced menu when you can carry packed lunch from home? Why would you want to sleep out in that fancy hotel room when your home is just but a stone throw away? Why would you save to purchase a car if you have no urgent use of it? And why would you insist on purchasing a car when you have no money to fuel it, service it or to money buy an insurance cover?

8. **Own your dwelling place**

   Own where you live. Or any amount of money you pay towards rent should be geared towards owning that house someday. Owning your place of dwelling won't only offer you convenience, freedom and peace of mind, but will equally help you free that *rent money* towards use in other projects such as savings, investments and or on other emergent needs.

9. **Shun the company of negative financial influencers**

Never be afraid of saying NO to unjustifiable financial solicitations, be it from close friends, relatives or colleagues. A famous connotation goes; *show me your bank account balance and I will show you your friends.* The world has conditioned us to "hang out" with people whom we fall in similar "classes of life". We consequently end up having friends whose earning and spending abilities are almost commensurate with ours. But there are some friends and colleagues who enjoy taking advantage of your financial innocence, and exploit you to their advantage. Those that take you out to the best hotel around for lunch only to end up making you pay all the bills. Those that lure you to purchase a personal car to take them out every weekends, while they purchase homes whose values keeps appreciating each month. While you are focused on pimping that car to match their taste, they on the other hand are working on acquiring a secondary house, or some parcel of land somewhere.

Hang out with people who respect your wallet. Your real friends respect your wallet. Avoid those crafty scavengers who retire to bed while scheming on how to extract money from you the next day. Avoid those night-club-thirsty brokes who don't even have a single cent to buy bottled water at that fancy night club they frequent courtesy of your wallet. Remember, such people will readily be around you when your life is filled with good fortunes, but you'll never see them during your financially trying times.

10. **Never lend money you can't afford to live without**

    Lending money to very close friends or relatives, especially to people who can easily take advantage of your generosity usually have ugly endings. Truth is it's never easy recovering money which has fallen in the hands of *a wrong borrower*. It's therefore vital to take you through some **Six Simple Safety Measures You Can Adopt To Help You Lend Your Money Safely**, if you must.

    ✓ **Only lend money you are willing to lose**

    If you are not willing to lose that money, don't give it away. If you can't live without that it, don't loan it out. It's that simple!

- ✓ **Establish the credit rating/credit score of the borrower**

    Technically, most individual lenders do shy away from taking this route, but in case you want to guarantee the safety of your money, simply ask the lender to provide you with his credit rating/score, obtained from a trusted credit reference bureau. This will help you establish if the borrower has any history of unpaid or defaulted payments.

- ✓ **Know basic details of the borrower**

    Know where the borrower lives, his/her permanent home address, some of his/her relatives, friends, family members etc. In case of default in payment or if inaccessible, you should know where or how to reach the borrower.

- ✓ **Ask for a guarantee or a guarantor**

    You can ask the borrower to provide you with some collateral. The value of collateral should equal that of the borrowed amount, or even higher. Equally, the borrower can have a reputable individual act as his/her guarantor. In case of any trouble in payment or total default in payment, you can turn to the guarantor for recovery.

- ✓ **Keep track of the borrower**

    You can occasionally call the borrower just to get to know how he/she is fairing on with life. You can equally occasionally call the guarantor, if any, to ascertain the wellbeing of the borrower. Don't wait for surprises.

- ✓ **And why not insure that money?**

    Practically, this might not be possible in several countries due to unavailability of relevant covers. Designing appropriate insurance covers for individual money lenders is literally an underwriting headache to many insurance providers. But if you come across an insurance cover which can shield you against losing money you are lending, go for it.

11. **Have an emergency kitty**

    An emergency kitty will always shield you from viewing credit as your safety net. And in the event of exposure to unavoidable life's emergencies or tragedies such as sickness, job loss, or death, you'll always have somewhere to run to for financial boost.

12. **Take good care of your health**

    There is a common saying that your health is your wealth. Go for those periodical checkups, eat healthy foods, stay on diet, drink lots of water, meditate often, do regular exercises etc. Do whatever you can to stay fit and healthy.

    And whatever strategies you adopt to help you earn money, ensure your health is never put at risk. After all, what would be the essence of acquiring all that wealth only to lose your life the next morning on avoidable health-related grounds?

13. **Always give back**

    You will never lack by giving. As a sign of gratitude, learn to give something to those less fortunate members of the society. Those who may never be in a position to pay you back.

    What special talent do you have? Can you find some time to mentor others? Use that unique gift you have to lift up or encourage others. When you freely give away, life will find a way of paying you back.

Key Points

Below are the thirteen financially healthy and highly rewarding habits you should adopt

1. *Live within your income*
2. *Establish other sources of income, and even more*
3. *Budget for every coin you earn*
4. *Save and invest part of your earnings, that windfall, that per diem, and that bonus*
5. *Avoid crowd-guided savings and investment approaches*
6. *Only get into debt you can afford*
7. *Spend more on items offering you savings on purchases*
8. *Own your dwelling place*
9. *Shun the company of negative financial influencers*
10. *Never lend money you can't afford to live without*
11. *Have an emergency kitty*
12. *Take good care of your health*
13. *Always give back*

Summary

To cure a leaking paycheck,

- Acknowledge that you are in a fix and in need of help, then seek for that help. Remember, if it has to be, it's up to you.

- Find some quiet space then list down all your debts. Clearly capture who you owe, at what rate and for how long.

- Involve your household and plan on fighting the debt as a team. Bring your household to a meeting and explain to them why the family's expenditure should be adjusted.

- Start with building an emergency kitty.

- Establish other extra sources of income.

- Organize the debts and begin paying them.

- Adopt the 13 financially healthy and highly rewarding habits.

www.ingramcontent.com/pod-product-compliance
Lightning Source LLC
Chambersburg PA
CBHW061159180526
45170CB00002B/866